THE VIVIAN POEMS

STREET PHOTOGRAPHER VIVIAN MAIER

BRUCE RICE

radiant press

Disclaimer: Although Vivian Maier was a real person, this is a work of fiction. Unless otherwise indicated, all the names, characters, businesses, places, events and incidents in this book are either the product of the author's imagination or used in a fictitious manner. Any resemblance to actual persons, living or dead, or actual events is purely coincidental.

Cover photo: Dean Bauche
Book and cover design: Tania Wolk, Third Wolf Studio
Printed and bound in Canada at Friesens, Altona, MB

The publisher gratefully acknowledges the support of Creative Saskatchewan and Canada Council for the Arts.

creative SASKATCHEWAN

Canada Council for the Arts | Conseil des Arts du Canada

Library and Archives Canada Cataloguing in Publication

Title: The Vivian Poems :Street Photographer Vivian Maier / Bruce Rice.
Names: Rice, Bruce, author.
Identifiers: Canadiana (print) 20200168533 | Canadiana (ebook) 2020016855X
| ISBN 9781989274293
(softcover) | ISBN 9781989274316 (HTML)
Subjects: LCSH: Maier, Vivian, 1926-2009—Poetry. | LCGFT: Poetry.
Classification: LCC PS8585.I128 V58 2020 | DDC C811/.54—dc23

radiant press
Box 33128 Cathedral PO
Regina, SK S4T 7X2
info@radiantpress.ca
www.radiantpress.ca

*To my sisters Connie, Lynne,
Kate, Jan, Megan*

Her Names

Dorothée *Viviane Thérèse Maier* (1926-2009). Vivian D. Maier on her 1950 passport which gives her occupation as a machine operator. Also known to use Miss Meyer, Miss Mayer, Miss Smith and Miss V. Smith. Vivian Maier in her obituary.

Preface

I try not to mind when others take photographs; I seldom take them myself. In quiet moments and the ones that really matter, I want to be fully present and to allow memory to do its work. It's a strange thing to say for someone whose writing is so thoroughly informed by art and photography in particular, and now I've written this book about a photographer. I still haven't figured out the contradiction. What interests me most is the artist, the thought and act of seeing, and how she came to that place.

I first heard about street photographer, Vivian Maier, when Stephen Bulger was interviewed on CBC Radio about a group of negatives he acquired for his gallery in Toronto. Maier worked as a nanny for well-to-do families in Chicago who knew little about her work, its variety and scope, nor the stunning images accumulating in Maier's room, in numerous stacks. Critics reference Lisette Model, Diane Arbus and Robert Frank when they speak of her. Her legacy of 140,000 black and white negatives, prints, undeveloped rolls of colour film, Super 8 films, and audio recordings were discovered in a Chicago storage locker auction in 2007. Two years later, Vivian died at age 83 in near-destitute conditions. She never benefited from the six books of photographs, two biographies, two feature documentaries, over 60 international exhibits, and now these poems.

Allan Sekula, the American photographer and critic, wrote that her subjects ranged "from down-and-out men in front of temporary employment agencies to the well-to-do parading on Michigan Avenue." She has been called an obsessively private person, which seems true enough, but some of her choices and mannerisms may have been reasonable and even necessary for her survival. It is not such a leap to imagine the child of a fragmented immigrant family, poverty and its persistent halo, and the simple fact of existing as a woman trying to make art. Vivian may have been self-taught but she was not a naïf. She was passionate about film and one of the finest galleries in the US was on her doorstep. She was a voracious reader. Ron Slattery, the first to buy her prints and put them on-line, said that her lockers held a huge number of books. There were many biographies and books on art. There should be little doubt that she understood how her work fit into its time.

In spite of the films, popular coverage and more serious studies, the pictures are the only documents we have that come directly from Vivian. I have taken license based on the few known facts. Some of these guesses may be correct, but they are fiction unless verified. More than anything else, these poems are a translation of what she left us. Vivian would object, but I hope they are as true to the art and who she was, as an artist, as such a thing can be.

Bruce Rice
Regina, Saskatchewan

Contents

PART IV THE SUPER 8 FILMS OF VIVIAN MAIER

PART V WALKING THROUGH

AFTERWARD

VIVIAN WRITES HER OWN PROLOGUE

Making a Spy

1

This is me ready
one needs to be ready.

This is my father
he leaves
with a suitcase
takes Charles with him.
Papa brushes me away
as if he were brushing dirt from his pants.
Charles' case strains, hits
the back of his legs so he pitches ahead
and now my father drags the tangle
of himself, Charles and the cases into the hall
the window over the stair squinting
as me and Maman watch them leave.

Are they leaving like
Papa says? Are we moving?

Pour un temps, Maman says.
For a while?
I'm not stupid
old enough to know half of me
is on one road, not a good one
and half of me is on another, also not good

and I recall quite clearly for all the things he did
this is when I decide to admire my mother less
and my father more.

2

This is me four.
Me, Maman and our bed in the apartment
of Jeanne Bertrand and her frayed
sapphire dress. She has a habit of looking
into reflections. White peonies laid
on the mahogany stand, her finger traces
the gleam on the table as if she were writing.
She's French like Maman, says
quite sternly I'm to call her *Madame*
which makes her chuckle when I do it.
We have a bit more food. Cream for tea
and mustn't waste it
sausages on Sunday.

Mme Jeanne, Maman
their stories slip into the space
under my door, like one wave
waiting for another. They think
I'm asleep, talk about men
Papa, of course
men married or single—no different.
Drawn up like a weight she's been reaching for
and finally found, Mme Jeanne says her secret
the baby she has given away, a boy. Like Charles.
I must be on guard.

3

I never knew people owned
more than one camera. Mme Jeanne
must be rich. The pantry is full of them, little machines
I look into and aim at her
but she's not smiling like I expected.
The walls have been cleared to the baseboards
to make room for photographs, black frames
in immaculate rows that round the corner—a surgeon
who never paid his bill, then a country doctor.
The one she likes best is three workmen
in clothes they wore that day.
She makes me guess *how old is this man* whose beard
uncoils like a white river with a shirt for a sandbar.
The women are different than Grand-Mère.
They face each other on opposite walls
and Mme Jeanne says she heard them whispering
just before we came in.
She means it.

It can't be real, a camera that fits
in a matchbox Mme Jeanne
folds it out like an accordion
but won't let me hold it.
For the rest of the month, I trail my fingers on the wall
and push the door as I walk by
but it's always shut. I never see her go in.
She calls me little Miss Mata
for Mata Hari which she explains
is a kind of spy-girl, so don't get shot.

The merry-go-round in Saint Mary's Park
knows me as Skinny Froggy, kids make this up then lick
the air with their tongues like they're catching a fly.
I never trust anything that can be taken away.
I have a name, Vivian. Is this true?
I haven't decided.

PART I

Necessary Questions

a slip of paper in a stack of self-portraits

says
light   *remember*

in a corner
I shield from the sun

so sudden   so deep
there is no place I cannot go

except for one I try not to think of

“happy” is such a meaningless word
everything casts a shadow

it’s all smoke and mirrors

mostly a mirror
what I ask is

don’t look at my legs
don’t look at my body

if I come close
don’t touch me

I’m not a planet
I’m not a pair of shoes

but maybe I am
maybe I am

A Necessary Question

What
makes us human
only a rich person
would ask such a thing
even an ant knows what it is
are you an ant

Maybe God put us here
maybe it's luck   I'm like
that Dane who deduced
how electrons work
that we can be streams
or waves at the same time

He kept a horseshoe over his door
Of course I don't believe in it he said
but I understand that it works
whether I believe in it or not

As for the world in six days—
from the shape we're in
I believe it
first we chip stones
attach them to spears
soon   given our nature
we'll blow ourselves to smithereens
we're no better than monkeys
digging with sticks

Does language make us smart
I've had better conversations with birds
than I have with some people
Better stick with the horseshoe

But humanity
that's the real question
I'm a difficult case myself
sometimes I wonder
why the universe bothers

I walk   I take pictures
with my beautiful *Rollei*
how many faces
pass through the lens
a thousand   ten
ten thousand faces!
I never thought to count the people
clinging to doorways
posts and each other

A Negro boy
wearing Mickey Mouse ears
looks directly into his future
a picture like this
fixes itself in your mind
but why

I should be terrified
I've seen
the tableau of an accident
certain appalling acts
but also
this exhausted
Canadian mother who cradles

her son   royal blue stag
knitted crudely into his siwash
blue for a sleeping boy
something his people
made by hand   his pretty mother
is not a Madonna   she'd be
a woman like me if I weren't single
I saw a statue with lines and a movement like this
in St. Peter's   the stone
transparent
this mother is too
but most of us don't think of ourselves
as works of art

My Rollei shoots from the waist
through it I see
like a child who's not very tall
and from whom much can be learned:

> digging graves is a job
> and often quite pleasant
> we seldom think
> of the birds and sunshine
>
> there are a few kinds of punishment
> a hundred kinds of shame
>
> whatever happens
> we cool off with Kool-Aid
>
> a man removing his shoes in a park
> is memorable

a boy who has never heard English can look
over broken slats of a fence   pickets topped
with peeling fluers-de-lis
and we can tell by his gaze that in some places
the only language left is on the graves

It's a full-time job
in some other life you can call me broken
but one thing I know:
water is a mirror
if in spring God
were to walk by a puddle in Battery Park
even He would pause to look at His reflection

But what could He do
there is too much to fix in ten thousand lives
all we can do is put up with it
it's why I never ask people to smile   myself
I don't ask for anything

Human River

Vivian Maier's New York Proof Sheets

the man in Bryant Park

I used to love
the snowy breath of Manhattan

the cloak
she drew about men like me

the wooden hearts of trees survive
this slush of age

the cold air has changed my lungs
a face in the skim of ice gapes back at me

I used to fly down a river
verglas so thin

if you stopped you'd break though
my scrolling blades flashed

like the backs of salmon
we chased upstream

this weather teaches
an avenue of empty benches

as younger men in better coats than mine
whisk by

I must look confused
as if I've arrived in someone else's future

its insouciant hour
and the remains

of a daydream no longer in love
with what lies ahead

drunk

man if I
was Stan Laurel
this'd be hilarious
creeps gawking
as this cop   nice cop tunic
leads me away

check out
my legs   scabs to the knees

my mouth
strangely has nothing to say
just a garbled complaint
sure I'll come quiet
whoever the hell you are
you're just one more stranger
who's done nothing for me

startled as I am
me 'n this cop
fall into a pose   arrested
by a novel kind of humiliation

narrow street in Sunset Park

Sunset Park boy
finds a way
to look in the box
left like a problem in front of a stoop
props this pallet
against it and stands on the slats   all he sees
is the shape of a mystery he can't reach

he doesn't have a ball glove
doesn't have a ball

so he patrols iron railings   parked cars
of cigar-smoking kings
and apartment lives
the ones you shock with the flash
of your intuition

remember Kirk Douglas crossing a street
a cop in the daylight   that woman collapsed
on an uptown street   newspaper
laid beneath to keep the filth off her clothes
these and other
accidental gestures of humanity

passengers

love   the world slows
for the phrase

of my snowy shirt   that shadow
in the cove of your throat

steel shoes of our dappled gray
ring on the avenue

in an open carriage
we are immaculate

framed in fenders of parked cars
in daylight drawn

from a modest star
whose far-removed planet

half-mystery
pushes off from the edge of the dark and the blue

its elliptical silence
a transit

our bodies studied so long
and still weren't prepared for

furniture mover

hey lady V

you're stuck in my mirror
don't worry lady
I'll get you out

and hey what's this –
a smile?
they said you had it in you
but I didn't believe them

still in the mirror?
put down that camera

smile lady V

in the viewfinder

two kinds of subjects: lookers
and watchers

sandbars that should be avoided
and depths you simply glide over

everything's balanced like this
two worlds to walk in

a city street
the human river

a domestic

washing windows
in her employer's brownstone
stands on the broad granite sill
rag in her hand as she reaches

over the open frame
which could be the bars of a cage
the poet warns   a thousand steel bars
and no world beyond

but humble or great   who's to judge
what poets know
of the light in the heart of a panther
or the contents of any life but their own

kiss

under the 8th street awning
we reach for each other

drawn and tormented
a small bright skiff

spun in the mouth of a river
when the gods are silent

we fall apart and dissolve
like pages of yellow fiction   the shambles

of everything we hoped passion would be
we've thrown our bodies away

the kisses we've bent
a crease   in the solitude

how Vivian sees it

—all of it
white-walled Lincolns
Lena Horne's light
Senegalese skin
Stormy Weather
in the great American
theatre of ourselves
in foyers of hotels
on stairs of the poor
who are too poor to die

this is the census
of the city's works
an homage to wreckage
her war on sobriety
cat eye glasses   mink stoles
and also the diary

of when she wasn't looking
when the bus didn't come
or the door of the change room swung open
and we saw her bra and naked back
this is her upskirt   the last hole in a belt
that can be tightened no further
this is how she looks with no mask

this is her one-man navy
this is her cop
this is the love she parks between two trees

this is her cigarette machine
venetian blinds opening   closing
like the eyes of a patient waking up from an operation
these murders
sex assaults
and holy waters
her Sisters of God   her sunny beaches'
rich people sleeping under umbrellas
these are the unmarked dead they'll become

sometimes she gets
married to Ash Can collectives
the art she looks at looks back
this is her light which digs its own grave
each dried ring of milk on the boarding house table
a sour aside
these are her Things with a capital *T*
this is her face refracted
these are the children of the grace she's abandoned
elegiac in their innocence
everything ends yet her task is endless
a paradox
and just to conclude my dear iron
park bench of Brooklyn
my dear Miss Quixote

I'm not your Sancho   I creak
and I turn
like the rest of your dreams

Chamsaur Valley, France 1950. Home village of Vivian's mother where the two lived, 1932-1938.

return to saint-bonnet

where I came awake
wondering how I managed to dream myself
into a valley   the precarious grace
of a girl not yet become
this storm of a body

I have heard of islands
where every leaving is an indelible grief
as if love itself has departed

valleys are like this

*

this audience of mountains observes me
no gesture too slight for their notice   the mountains are in me
the height doesn't matter

the village cross seems a small thing
a darkly faithful marker in all this unreachability
the sky above us   argent in winter
cobalt in spring
but our place is the valley
the mountains' atoms carried in streams
we drink the minerals
then shade our eyes and gaze hopefully into the sun
like fruit trees waiting to blossom
the roofs of Place du Chevréril

pitch steeply in the background of wedding pictures   a sunlit
glint of corners to illuminate gravestones and the poses

of agreeable old men
the south wall of my house
is flocked like canvas
before it I've seen
I could be pretty

when the shadow of a cloud crosses the pass
you can see deeper into it
I've climbed there before   the thin air
makes me breathe more deeply until I get used to it
this is how mountains take your measure

but it's only a gesture
an exhilaration I know
but not belonging to me

Smile

1

Before they speak
people who don't know me smile anyway

There's nothing of theirs I can take
the poor always surprise
with their good cheer

This Saint-Bonnet girl with hazel eyes
clings to her dolly
I speak French in that
come-along voice my mother used
(where did that come from)

The child finally smiles   an honest one
the world hasn't reached
one of the lucky few
who wear no mask

2

An auburn-haired mother
looks into my Rollei
her daughter   and even the baby
seem skeptical

and it's not that this woman's life is set
she looks in my eyes

the smile's not for me
it's for them
they don't even see it

3

People like to show their teeth
gold ones
chipped or stained   scored even
a farm hand   looks up as he pours milk
into a gleaming separator

lucky teeth
buck teeth
young girls in calico

sometimes I think I could lift
what they lift squinting into the sunlight
a doorframe
to hold up a smile

4

I'm often cast
as today's glad adventure

some of them fret
about the end of the month
bastard men
and who I am
they'd rather not bother
ashamed to be

unfit citizens of this
poor but happy Earth

5

I envy the grace
of these *femmes* **âgées**
how dreary   those snapshots
(you know the ones) of "rustic lives"
"the wisdom of age" et cetera

themselves they would laugh *La sagesse*
c'est pour les prêtres
a face is a face   and it's hard to say
who has lived well and who simply waits
for the final punctuation

6

It's not mine to say
who is more honest
the person who's happy
or the one who never is

I never smile for a camera
smiles are for family albums
but some days I find
a luminous thing

this beautiful Malayan
smiles with her skin
I've bought
her camphor wood box

she waits by a stall
where honey's heated and thinned
how patient she's been   a smile
to recall when I'm home
beneath the dome of a formerly grand station

or in some ancient place where the rain
has stroked the walls smooth

Pigeon Boy

I tell him
hold the bird higher
I see right away he's experienced at this
Fingers stroke the indigo sheen
made mostly of air   an avian furnace
cupped in his hands

Something I see in his unresolved smile
Is this how you want me to look he says
but of course I don't want him to look
any particular way

Of all the boys in the park
he is himself
different and strange

He cocks his head   a look
I understand is a judgment
a companion whose gaze does not falter

In the Maloof film, Finding Vivian Maier, a linguistics professor calls Maier's French accent "an affectation."

On the Idiolect of V

Disingenuous in that voice
you exhale over your students
Professor you denounce
my vowels   *too long for French*

Children who know me
say I speak like I'm about to sing   maybe it's true
I've heard quite a few people
singing on Maxwell Street   a cappella
there are a million ideas of language

Take a child
born in New York
her mother abandoned
in a family tradition of such abandonment
the Depression not yet hit bottom
She takes her daughter home
to Saint-Bonnet-en-Champsaur

Under the mountain of France the girl must construct
her own floating island on the lake you call language
she pulls sounds from the air
the way birds imitate other birds or perhaps
the girls of École Rue 8 Mai

She is making her own girl-country
and what would she choose   carts
trundling the bucolic lanes of Saint-Bonnet
a green mountain pasture with sun on its steeples

Or the throb of New York's
Gospel of Market   the whole country quoting
O say can you see   as her waters
shift to questions of skin

tract houses in deserts that *will not be moved*
her electrified criers of blues
plugged into the crosshairs of Halsted and Maxwell

How could a girl learning to speak
make her way in that country
alone with that dark thing
that makes her careful with men

Professor you should know
we are all a stranger to someone
as for language
I had none in Saint-Bonnet
so I began to compose a little song
that happened to throw its halo around me
I decided then
this is how I should speak

Speaking of Shadows

I keep the sky behind me
I am either 5’8
or six feet the children say
my height keeps changing just after 4:00
when the sun starts sinking

This is not their nanny’s day off
I work
at what I find eloquent
which is just about everything

Light on the wall
the lake beyond
what does it harbor
I am speaking
of what signs point to

As for my sentences
kind of like singing
it’s how I conduct myself

PART II

Nothing Wasted

the children
I care for: sleeping
in cribs, discovering
their shadows
putting on
their pajamas
showing their bruises
these negatives
I mark “Les Enfants”
classify some
assez
bon / rather
good

Let me explain about legs

for example this mother's
grip on her daughter's shoulder

on a succinctly clipped lawn
suburban they stand
halfway into their fate
or if you don't believe in fate
then what is to come

*

a girl draws herself up on tiptoes
her fingers can't reach
the postcard display

her pink barrette
her sunny sundress
can't make her taller

her brother   her father
turn their backs
she already knows what not to ask for

things are ignored until they disappear
this is the dictionary of their family

*

two artists *en plein air*
the slender one's legs
the careful proportions of her body
the man with her   poised

like a heavy tear with a belt cinched round its belly
though who can say what the proportions of their lives are
usually it's the man who is happy

*

conversation is a corner   two women
in heels and one in flats
the story flows easily
the third one is anxious

behind Givenchy sunglasses
a fourth woman turns   nervously touches
the dusky skin of her shoulder

a study in frailty
and the kind of intimacy
in which she will always be other

*

my legs? I show only
to myself

*

I'd rather see *him*
the parcel he holds by the string
and how desperately he protects it

I know the story   heelless socks
shoes like this live in the park
hang off the end of a bench
or the end of a stretcher
it's not a disguise

*

no lovers no fares
so the carriage driver waits
at a shoe shine   no school for the boy
dipping his brush in polish

the boy is poor
the driver broke
and the horse must be looked after

*

    split jump over
    Central Park trees
    Cossack dancer's arms push
                the walls
    of the temple apart
    as he flashes his most
    disarming grin

    Samson's last day
    must have been good

*

a scavenged pigeon
curled by the drain

or legs of a vagrant who sleeps
like a corpse from a battle
with one arm still raised
whatever it held has escaped

*

legs
in tantrum

or quietly scuffing feet glimpsed in the gap
under the Blue Line fence
shopgirls and men in creased suits   discreetly
eyeing each other between someplace
and home

looking at legs
you see things like this

an eccentric language you think you should know
its strange punctuation

*

people who hate
to be photographed
never argue when you take pictures
of their legs

which may be bandaged
or caked   a nanny
clutching a squirming child

a leg in a week-old cast   singular

legs dashing into water
mannequins in storefronts articulated
to indicate their lyric gaze

tanned soles of lovers
sprawled under the Wilmette Park boardwalk
or a family tableau at the CTA bus

we are incomplete
in the manner of the Elgin marbles
all the poses of the human temple
delivered in silence
like a Valentino tango
so lyrical
and yet so apocryphal

perhaps I'm a flâneur
a passionate wanderer
or an idiot
encyclopaedic
in the scope of her appetite
but my intention is serious

I humbly submit
this anatomy of walking

3:00 PM in a Quiet Station

are you too early
have you come late

show me the moment
when you can be seen

I think and I think of all the little pictures
hung on your wall   the address

of your heroes
your hallowed dead   halls

lined with paintings of flowers transplanted
from notions of landscape

here's the strand of a dream someone
brushed from your face   I ask nothing but this

of all you sleeping little princes
all you waiting long-haired girls

Somewhere

my father's alive
he's that kind of man

the last I heard my brother
calls himself Charlie

or William
when he needs it, what he's become

so much salt in the ground
and Maman whispering

This can't be
This can't be

I'm not ashamed
to be alone

there's only one thing
you can say

to a girl who's brought home
at the wrong time

to the wrong people
when she's old enough tell her

make up a story, true in some ways
even to her

the age of reason is seven
when she sees their life

sees how it is, tell her firmly
you are seven years old

you are a girl, you must
save yourself

To Her Young Charges

Girls

it will happen   a man
who comes into your home

an uncle brings presents
something cheap and jokey
he will swing you up
and give you rides on his knee
                    ride a cockhorse to Banbury cross
                    baa baa black sheep
he'll tickle you in front of everyone
until you kick the floor
it's *so* funny

then one day he's bouncing you on his leg and he
reaches
under your shirt
he'll pretend not to notice
I assure you   he does
you'll feel something poky in his lap and one time
he won't let you off   he's not
laughing this time he's saying
a secret   your mother
is really really poor
and might have to send you away
he could help   but your mother worries
she is so poor
you are so bad
I assure you he'll think of something while he keeps
poking you as much as he can
I'm not making it up

Nothing Wasted

I'm one of those creatures
that carries their life with them
a system of books, the *Times*
by week
month
year.
I need it in reach
the news is like water
if no one reads it
it evaporates.

I save these bags
I'm quite poor myself
I don't waste anything.
What you learn is
things must be sorted
a useful thing wasted
carries a levy of shame.

The thing is the pictures, easy
to lose: graves in Saint-Bonnet
society wives in new
fall dresses, the touching way
they hesitate on sidewalks in a half-second of sunlight
when nothing's decided.

I keep thinking back
to that poor dead cart horse stripped of harness
and pulled off the road, the fading
chestnut sheen of the colt she was, eloquent
the only natural thing on the street.

Things show up—a black man quietly
brushing up litter in the gleam
of expensive cars.
And I love how wind off the lake
makes lawyers on Madison clutch their coats
the *Hawk* they call it; and November's
gilding 4:00 o'clock light.

I go to galleries when it's free. People pretend
they're looking but that's not the world.
All I can do is save the pieces
I'm not even sure I chose this vocation.
You can't frame your own life
but you feel the weight of things.

Maxwell Street: Letters from a Bazaar

1

Sunday saves me, Maxwell and Halsted
the sizzling onions, Polish sausage, Vienna red hots
and these pullers working their chatter *o we got shirts o*
we got hats for a dollar sir you look good but a one dollar hat
very sharp sir very sharp … ma'am how can you let him walk
around without a good hat…how 'bout socks four for a dollar
the only hole is the one you put your foot in …a one dollar hat
and I'll throw in two pairs of socks you're killin' me sir you really
are killin' me…. miss lookit we got fifty-cent blouses for you 'n
your sister… your daughter? I thought you was sisters…ladies
lookit the seams …any cheaper and I'd have to fire myself
you know you need gloves miss…miss…

Not lies when everyone knows it, just a patois
that's met its master.

2

I come as early as the train can get me here. People need
to make money, no time for church and anyway
Maxwell has forgiven more people than Saint Francis.
You see their empties Italian Swiss Sherry—the creatures
who drank it hide in doorways as if the sun hurts their skin,
drifters in hope of a spot in Hell that's a little less worse than
the day before. Sid Goldstein says when a worm crawls in a
radish and he's never known anything else, then for all he
knows he's in a peach. I don't believe it. They know.

3

God, if there is one, must be a Democrat. Just look
at these Independent Baptists with more starch
and more white in their faces than on their shirts,
but there's no doubting their luminous intensity and if it isn't
coming from The Bible then it's coming from somewhere.
They claim there are angels among us. The man in the thin
olive suit beside me gives me a nudge, says
The only angels I know are in Heaven. I never seen
an angel on this Earth. Not one.

I like the Black choirs better. They seem to think you've
already been saved, it just hasn't occurred to you yet.
Your bones believe it, a voice rising out of the flesh of itself,
it only wants to be what it is, singing and stomping and calling,
an instrument doing its work.

4

Louis H. Sullivan never lived here.
Frank Lloyd Wright put his bungalows
out in the country, not here.
Jimmy's Hotdog Stand is open all the time, however.
Lou Fish can sell you any kind of silk and Rooftop Brown
will chase a burglar though any place a human being can go.

No rags-to-riches or pull yourself up
by your second-hand bootstraps here, but Rooftop
can show you it flows: Jews who landed too poor
for stores downtown so they set-up here or on Halsted
then Irish, then German, Mexicans, Blacks with no choice—
Chicago so much better than the sunny South and Jim Crow
or braceros pulling sugar beets, picking California peaches.

The Defender said it was here
If you want a job
If you are having trouble with your employer
If you want a place to live

Or they came from close in—
town population 378 with no work
so change your life, go to school
fall in love and keep going
regular stories about regular people, nothing so tragic
or noble with chapters in books running after them.
As for the rest: born here, lived here, died here.

5

A kid with twenty wind-up bullfrogs lined up on a box.
"They'll go all day," he says.
"Have you tried them yourself?"
"Sure," he says, "I'm here all day
and they've been with me the whole time."

6

Talking last week to this man I usually talk to, he asks
if I have fifteen cents so I give it to him.
He has no socks like so many of these down-and-out
fellows. The smell is quite rank but still, apart from
some soap and water how are his bare feet so different
than my bare feet, and I have to wonder
what this "same cloth" is we're all supposed to be made of.

Boards laid across sawhorses one day a week
piles of toilet seats, rain coats, tchotchkes and tinny pictures
of Pope Paul VI—if the City doesn't shut it down
this is work: trying to make the short end of the stick
a little bit longer.

7

Better roll them dice
Better roll them right
If I catch you cheatin'
Gonna take your life

That would be Blind Arvella Gray, he's here hollering
every Sunday, though he never says his real name or tells
the same story twice. First, he says he was a getaway driver
for the Purple Gang and got two fingers shot off in a botched
stick-up, which is why he only plays slide guitar.
The next week he says a jealous husband shot them off.
It's just as likely the police got one finger and the husband
got the other, but who wants to encourage such a terrible liar.

8

A good eye—you need more than that.
People come with their cameras,
they think it's exotic.
The hawkers and pullers
put up with it: attention has its uses.

If I had a family album
this would be it, people who know me.
The Sistine Chapel hasn't seen half the things
this place has. No one wants it—not the Mayor,

the police or the Burnham Plan. People
made it anyway and kept it going, suspended it from wires:

chaotic
and elegant,
a savant junkman's mobile art made from parts
he built himself. It moves the world when you wind it up.

caught at last
                                                  the rain

the common backyard birds' airy tumult
as sewer grates mouth surprise

leaves refill themselves   crisp lit edges gone
dull drops on dull chrome

everything that takes a breath speaks at once

a thrush's gangly silhouette in the gingko tree
as the bird takes cover

the air a mineral

as an empty swing cups what falls
has already fallen

florets tumbled white from lilacs
as paths unscroll in paintings of

the last words of leaves

PART III

1968

If this hope were to be brutally destroyed a new kind of massacre of innocence would have occurred... I think the sense of tenderness we have experienced would readily become a source of danger for the whole country.

– Studs Terkel

Vivian on the Shooting of Dr. King

Even in our sleep, pain which cannot forget
falls drop by drop on the heart
until in our despair, against our will
comes wisdom through the awful grace of God.

> *Robert Kennedy quoting Aeschylus as he breaks the news of the death of Martin Luther King to a crowd in Indianapolis.*

1

How tall can we make
the letters in a word

I cannot move
the *Times* stacked so deep in my room

I can't reach my bed
so I sleep on the floor

sifting a question:
what kind of country are we

flag-wrapped idiots who dream up things
to wring the country with? *assassinate*

too small a word for what's in our throats
even in our sleep, pain which cannot forget

2

I warn the children
stay clear of me today

but the sidewalks already know
the song, the one about monkeys

jumping on a bed, one falls off
and bumps his lovely head

it's all so simple
we've heard rifle fire before

and this inhalation before the elegy, as grief
falls drop by drop on the heart

3

Faces today
on the Loop moved me

resistance
moves me

outside their make-shift churches
what I heard moved me

dragged to jail, they sang or kept on
I was humbled in hope and in loneliness

I'm not a marcher though I try to believe
in *the urgency of now* like King said

and that *unearned suffering is redemptive*
but what if

there's only the great Until
until in our despair, against our will

4

What kind of people are we
Bobby spoke

from the deck of a flatbed truck
all it took was the question

people needed to hear
I don't know who Aeschylus was

except
his tragedies came in threes

no one is spared and it's only a hope
with suffering

comes wisdom
through the awful grace of God

After the riot

Chicago West Side after the shooting of Martin Luther King

1

too expensive to be ashamed
cameras detest
and love this

a *War Zone*
a word to attach
to the six o'clock news
Black Panthers
juvenile youth
the blacks and their gangs
six o'clock faces explain

but gangs don't do this
two miles of Madison gone
flags downtown   at half-mast for King
or maybe for this
pathetic

my cover is *a nanny riding alone*
past basements still smoking
as walls kneel into them
no flags here   but the bus still runs
gasping at each stop in the weird silence

whites take seats by themselves
read the *Tribune*   or stare out the window
it was no easy dream some lunatic ended

2

At California & Madison
I get out and walk west
other women walking as if they are lost   there's
something

they urgently need but can't think what
it's a strange addiction   I look in the remains of houses
people still believe if there is no photograph
it didn't happen   funerals
weddings   and *this*

it's foolish to think my camera
will keep me safe

two boys on bikes
dressed quite neatly   one says
we just wanted to see
ten years old but now
it's the place where the memory happened
shoes   bloody clothes
caps in the park and everything left behind

3

I keep my nerve
I know what moves me

a yellow backhoe with its scoop
on the ground
a posture of mourning
that both is   and isn't true

except for their reflex in front of a camera
not smiling no   two city workers eating a sandwich
they seem relaxed
there's no hurry and some jobs
never get done

outside her store this white woman poses
her grown son too
as if they're in prison
they don't know what they'll do
it's calm but maybe the West Side is not done erupting

and they're slaves with no way to flee this bewildered
Roman holiday town
mother and son   food for the ashes

4

the poor I know work all the time   three jobs at least
hawking in stalls in December
boiling or freezing
cleaning hotels
do I need to describe it:
picturesque faces which left to themselves would say
we're fed up

the cities *on fire*
are really on fire

a committee can't fix it
maybe they'll shoot and maybe they won't
this is the terrible flaw of a lie
and what it looks like

Robert Kennedy

June 5, 1968

It can't seem
To let itself end, children in bed
Papers quote one another
And come up with nothing that hasn't been said
24 years since Normandy, but today missed the beach
And landed in some hotel in L. A.
We're broken so bad we can't even weep
For the hero, the elegized dream
Our dream took root in, a thing we'll never get back

He was in charge… When I walked away from Daley's office, I thought, 'We're going to have violence. He's going to unleash his Police Department.' Richard J. Daley was the embodiment of power so tightly wrapped up in its own righteousness that it couldn't hear any words echoed back but those words that are echoed back from his own mouth.

—Roger Wilkins, US Justice Department, on the Chicago Democratic Convention, August 26-29

Vivian with her charge, Inger Raymond, during a pause in the protests, Chicago Democratic Convention.

Watching Us

Little Inger is afraid
the police will kill us

The world tuning in must wonder
what planet we live on
an eerie radiance at night
men with nightsticks and gas masks
coming out of the fog

This college boy sleeps
sitting up on a bench
face in his hands
I've seen beggars do this before

His friends' bedrolls
lined up on the lawn   respectful
as if it were summer camp

Richard J. Daley
one of the titans
a phone strike   the electricians strike
stopping the news and cameras looking in

The world is watching us
From the 25th floor of the Hilton
Hubert Humphrey
surveys a scene from some other country

Tear gas   police
the Vietnam War come home
first King
then Bobby
this feels like one more funeral
the elegy's garbled
and words won't redeem us

This bench
is where people meet when they have nothing left
I need pictures
but my heart has gone out of it

I say Inger let's go   let's find
that red coat of yours   pretend it's winter
and snow has covered us up
let's say the crashing and chants are a band
practicing on Soldier Field
and the megaphone's warning is part of a game
that goes back and forth until we fall down
laughing till our sides ache

and this bench is grateful
to have served its purpose
a place to see things
and reflect on them
and bring them out like a photograph
when reflection is missing
and we can't quite remember the day

PART IV

The Super 8 Films of Vivian Maier

They Could Be Vivian

Film 1   Mystery Mink Coat Woman

It's too warm
for my coat   my lipstick
might be smudged
but time
is what's urgent
so much and no more   to catch
the walk light
a month
to my anniversary
twenty-five years   that's a mortgage
but my hair color
will get me through
my address
Highland Park
my situation's
a blur
peripheral like this flower bed
or lines
on the road
things you think about later
I know you are looking
because of my style
because it is me
it's not your fault
you want
to see me
but now
I really must go
it's time I must go

Film 2 Woman with Shopping Bags

Two grocery bags
white babushka
a good wool coat
(she gets cold easily)
men from the construction site
step to the side
even they know the trajectory
she's still coming from
gleaning what's left
of smoldering fields
and a village close to the border
ground on which innocence
is no defense
fifty-four years since she landed
English is her passport not her country
these men
nod
as she passes
this is not their space

Film 3 Camera Boy, Incident Girl

Him:

Kids like to touch
the candy red ambulance six cops
slide some guy in handcuffs into the back I missed
the whole thing and this leg cast
sure doesn't help

I like all this seeing again and again
the weirdness
the way people stand about when something bad happens
and they've nothing to do: *it's not our show*
we're only the extras lined up at the gate

I'm not sure it's worth wasting film on
I've heard everything we do from now on
will be shown millions of lives watching millions of lives
until nice people can't even see what they're looking at
accidents or pretty girls
that's not for me I want
the story we almost know
no one can say where to look
but I'm starting to find it

Her:

I must write this down, the way I stand very still in my mind, like a woman with pearls who looks out from a softly lit canvas as time carries on. And how strange, this boy and Miss Meyer (?) from down the block filming the crowd and each other. I do this too in my journal, stories where one spirit slips into another.

He's cute on those crutches. I like the sly way he watches like he plans to be famous. It's a kind of pose that doesn't know it's a pose. He's oblivious like most boys, *stranieri in amore con se stessi e le stelle*, my mother says—young men are strangers in love with themselves and the stars.

Even with his back turned, he knows I am here. Someday I must show him how beautiful and deceptive a word can be.

F2 Tornado:
Roofs torn off frame houses; mobile
homes demolished; boxcars overturned
large trees snapped or uprooted; highrise
windows broken and blown in;
light-object missiles generated.

Film 4 Tornado Woman

dodges what's left
as shards of expensive colonial shutters
shrapnel the ground
elms snapped   Tornado Woman
steps up for a look in the windows
of a ripped house

how fashionable
her red coat waving against a flat white thing
people lived in
her hips
direct one way
her head points the other
now you can see what she's aiming for   clearly
an amateur
she films
so she can say later
she was here when it happened
neither model nor housewife
she's detached
from disaster

the wind's shredded path
Earth's skin split
Appalling the News says
21 Palm Sunday killers   tornadoes
and yet in the wreckage
a space

we cannot deny   our attraction
to a red coat bobbing

Film 5 Slide Girls

On the pile
that *was* a house, two girls

take turns, slide down the roof
on a baby's rubber mattress, squeal and run back.

Three more girls check out the ruins.
What else should they do? Parents have rules

for spring coats, white or grey. Mothers braid
their daughters' long hair. There are no rules for this.

They float above the skyline—five young swans
in a back-lit ballet. But still, being real live girls

they have to work out who's the responsible one
and who'll be the baby.

Across town, in khaki Stetsons, two state troopers
guard the remaining half of a Texaco station.

They're here to make sure no one
blows himself up stealing gas, four letters left

on the torn sign behind them. In yards'
shredded cosmos—a sputter of wires.

No matter how strange
five girls at play

is consoling, their faith in something
that wasn't meant for us as if this were only

the wind in the night, a change
nothing more than the long wait for Spring.

Film 6 Gatherer

I'm not the teacher. All I know is ages ago a river came by, making this place hidden from suburbs and plans, a pocket of grass sprinkled with berries to collect in paper cups. *Ravine*—the sound of the word is a groove that widens into a sunny afternoon with no motives: better than Eden, a real, overlooked place where girls don't worry about a bit of mud on their skirts and the smallest boy wears a woodsy cap from Sears. They're careful not to step on the wine-colored runners and clusters of saw-toothed leaves covering the strawberries. I never say I'm their nanny, a word I refuse. As for my life, this is the one I wanted. I'm quite plain, really, but I've made it this far; I have found a place that brushes my skin. It vibrates. Children kneel and their knees leave small prints in the ground as if they were deer. They lick their stained fingers. If they were seeds they would whirl a bit but this is where they would come to; if they were clouds, this is where they would drift.

Film 7 Stock Yard Girl

Inger holds her nose for the camera, Vivian
laughs—it's a movie set main street
with hogs coming through, signs swing
Stockyard Inn, Sirloin Room
and *Stockyard Grill* in big block letters

This could be a *Miss Maier Adventure*
Inger's red coat, a flash of color
to draw the eye
from the stink, filth that clings to the windows
like a fog made of animal sweat or the animals themselves

Miss Maier leads on—no visitors here
no school tour as dazed sheep peer
between slats of a liner, a carcass casually
tossed on the ground
death is the push of everything here

In the cowshit and chaos
a Red Angus bull mounts a heifer, probably figures
it's what he's here for

*

Fifty years later
the stockyard gate is a monument, this film scrap
of Inger's red coat
and that inert sheep
a record

With a farm and grown children
all Inger can say is
What kind of crazy woman
would do such a thing
I could tell stories…

"Chicago murder of mother and baby, market where she found add [sic] for babysitting job which led to disappearance and death." (Vivian's handwritten note on a Super 8 film cartridge.)

Film 8 The West Ardmore Girl

A deer will sniff a carcass
to learn how it died.
What does one animal feel
when an animal of another species dies?

Here at the store where it started
a guard dog—a pet, really—
suns himself on the gravel roof, a witness
to deeds of no concern to him: the Ardmore girl's
path across the parking lot, how intently
she focused, shifting her purse
as she copied the note on the bulletin board—
an easy trail to follow now, but that afternoon
instinct failed.

*

Let's walk into the story, although like most characters
we don't know it's a story.

We lead mostly good lives but there's always
that sense of our own disguise
and the hubris of the world.

*

At Ardmore and Meade:
the boundary you crossed
when you followed her here
her last street, last crosswalk, last

steps, windows of the apartment
it happened in. Many stories end like this.
Newspapers shout at the shape
they can't figure out, it's murky
and there's no help for it—the sirens
the sensation, the ponderous machinery
that keeps us here
and our own low place.

*

Outside the funeral home, two women work out
what they'll do later. The service is over
but it wasn't for her—the Ardmore girl—
nor anyone we know.
What she could afford
you could put in an envelope.
These women are here for the story, an arc
once begun that never touched ground.

To lose.
What we have lost. At the end of the tour we don't
know what happened, which leaves us

to the closing of eyes we loved, their cool
receding and this worn coin
of the sorrow we know
which at least
is honest.

Film 9 Citizenship Day Parade Assembly Area

we the assembled clowns
in red pantaloons, welcome you
to an imagined country

of golden banners, where always
the youngest brother overcomes
with the power of innocence

and tales of the char girl, who
in persecution
is revealed a princess

Liberty leads our procession
poofed purple hair, horn-rim glasses; just now
she's having a snort in back of a half-ton

she was almost sold off for scrap, you know
and that Emma Lazarus poem
wasn't till later

*

middle-aged Soldiers of the Revolution
pass cigarettes and sip bourbon
from Dixie cups, funny guys

but rather good-looking in those tricorne hats
another year's strain on their buttons
they have that swagger

of men together, heroically
covered in mist, waiting to stride
into the weather of their serious intent

*

Clydesdales shake their traces and wait, no hurry
to draw a custard-yellow wagon crowned by six idiots
who practice elaborate bows to lukewarm applause

we, the assembled clowns
have many hours to consider
corned beef on rye at Baker's Lunch

we are honest purveyors of hoopla
ever alert to an attractive widow
buying digestive cookies

or this couple, one of them reaching for the other
in a chill wind, their corner drama
pulled by its edges

*

something they've found in the gutter, two kids
leap high off the curb, stomp on upended
drink cups with a satisfying *pow!*

we clowns invite you
to climb to any high place
a park bench, a lamppost

we run through the crowd
with an improvised shtick, trade
your hat with ours and won't give it back till you sing

the hour of the clown has come
it always does, and this
my good Pagliacci, is *It*

PART V

Walking Through

a boy in the branches

I don’t have to ask
you know where to look

how to hide
without seeming to

you were born knowing
how to amuse

if I had a son
he would not be you

if I had a girl
she would not be me

the rare thing you’ve learned
is to let the day go

things I say you will not remember
what is true now may not always be true   but they say

when you look at a photograph of a person
you can love that person

this is in us
it does not disappear

Twins, Florida

There once was a tree
A pretty little tree
The prettiest tree
You ever did see

This is what the sun has done
with crinoline dresses   the twins'
tousled hair   and two identical strings of ten-cent pearls

This is no trick
the breeze neatly folding a collar
the dazzling brims of their sun hats

I'll shoot no more today
I've done enough and besides
some drinks are so cool you don't need more

I have no sister to pull on the wishbone
which breaks it of course
which is why I don't wish

But these girls' freckled skin
some days a light touch is all you need
to know you've been touched

Scene at the Beach

                                    This all-
American youth in a one-piece
pin-up girl pose, her laughter's
an anthem.
She could be Norma Jean
with real blond hair
maybe Athena
come out from her temple.

She lies in the sun like a piece
of marble still in the quarry   her lover
up in the beach house   pours a tall blue
cocktail   and like those Italian tombs
where the dead recline in glistening repose
she does not sleep   but rather
makes a shroud of a towel
and covers her face.
Between the precise wheeling of terns
and the rumored sea
a summons
a hiss.

Undersea Restaurant

                                        Faux velvet
seats. Two dyed carnations gripped
in a vase   as this son of Neptune
swims to my window   hair dazzling
like seagrass. He's
checking me out.
Buoyant force pushes
him up or perhaps
all this is sinking.
I'm ready to eat
the house wine tastes great
and for once the throb in the darkness
is only the sea.

Pluviophile

a soaked road is a soaked road
rain is rain
there's nothing wrong
with a pile of wet lumber
nothing

this is the scene   my bag on the ground
bike held up   by the kickstand

a fine rain out in the open
the skin of what's really here

Three Windows

1

this is not the night I was ready for
I was waiting

for a meditation on Christmas tree lights
in silenced windows

not this unreadable dark in the yard rising out of me
how shall I get up tomorrow

and in the evening when I've done
all of tomorrow's things

return to this
a few empty stars

2

where nothing else is   one thing
is something   a stop sign

the moon moored behind it
drawn in with pencil

3

I look into myself a corner window
the light left on

like a footlight after the play
its stories done

which makes room for new ones
this is what a dream is

a space in a light
with nothing in it

4

the dark
and three windows

not connected to anything
why should they care

for an eloquent ending
they're nothing these eyes

Winter View from an Elevated Train

in the saddle between peaks   from the Strauss
to modern Water Tower Place inured to the season

human lights
shine through the crosshatch

we wrap our faces but it does no good
the cold sees us and the wind finds us

we speak in short breaths
that come out of our mouths and hang there

cathedrals wait for a Tiffany sun
so we may speak

of valleys again   moraines the maps call suburbs
and our paths between them

Proofs of Winter

1

Snow

nothing more
as cracks in the walk show through
like veins under skin   a sign
for the kind of intimacy that buries its scars
slips beneath the talk talk talk
and finds its way
a kind of rest

like spaces left in the tracks of birds
without loss
without words

2

Two resolutions:
to look out the window more often
to know the difference
between smalt blue
and cobalt which came later
and how the colors we invent
are still true colors
known all along to the first light that hits them

and so it seems to me my pictures of things
are true things
real as ice
on a clump of hawthorn berries
the same ruby flesh
the same burden

3

Between storms
wings lift the intentions of birds   a whirr
of precision as roofs disappear
in snow-piled planes pierced by a steeple
the iron bell stilled to a kind of perfection

an assurance in the heart there is such a thing
a kind of ease

4

Things I know
I know by walking through them
this is why we have seasons
our strangeness is
to want to see what is new as the world
comes out of darkness
sometimes a cirrus wisp in a deep sky   blooms
and fills with itself
pushed
as I am
when I am walking through—to the end of it
and if this wind with its reasons takes me
then we are even

To the 12,000 Unmarked Graves Under Lincoln Park

hallowed the bones
beneath my feet   these catholic dead
a footing for the Archbishop's house

hallowed the dog that walks here and the roots   grave-fed
of the grass it walks upon

and the obvious invocation
accrues
in the intersection of Goethe Street
and Sandburg Terrace   a misty
salutation to the poets' insistence
and this civic imagining of who we are
and will be   and the naivety
of such naming

hallowed this seeing
of the crescent lakeshore even though I grumble
in the city that saved me
though nothing biblical

Chicago
with the vibration of trains
traversing her corpus   not a saint
but maybe a venerable who can at least intercede

I get her news   I love her fight
the Tribune and I read her Defender
its black ink's resistance   inscribing
either freedom exists or does not

no in-between
I came here to work   I'm not sure what I'm owed
but the lake made the wind
and this town made a space I can live in

old men sleep—hallowed
on the grass in Lincoln Park
I try not to disturb them   or what lies beneath

who knows if they're poor   or simply tired and do this
because this is how they want to be old

they don't think of me watching   they don't think of
the light   falling defiantly on them
some day I'll lie down like this
grass will grow
Lincoln Park will go on
and her lovely saints too

this is such a strange day to think of these things
the generous dead   this mishigamaa
a lake
a thought or kind of seeing
that has no shore except the last one   and that
well-known to sleeping men

mishigamaa: an Anishinaabe word meaning "large water" or "large lake". The French word is "Michigan".

Under the Sassafras

V at 82

it’s not so bad to be left on a bench
with green waves above you

today I walk safe
in my mother tongue

the boards of memory
doing their job six months more.

When these little falls
put themselves together

sit by the lake
never curse things there’s no help for

be as small as you really are
talk to the shore.

EPILOGUE

Intestate

Call me Viv, Vivian, Miss Maier
or spy

take me for the names I go by, the version
you loved or didn't.

I'd scatter all of it
this chatter, and tomorrow you'd see

I have moved a few inches
some piece of me.

It comes down to ashes.
If it's ashes

it's only the heart's grey inflections
quite grainy   with ten thousand faces looking this way.

I leave you the audacity
what I saw every day

and goes on being
whether I am here or not.

This is a key
myself on paper blown about

worthless as that.
Leave it to the dust

I was almost gone anyway
and I was never that heavy

none of us are
so we may be lifted

and of all the things in the world to be seen
that moment remembered

how we spoke or walked or slept
our common selves worn like a coat

incorruptible as any saint
because we *are* remembered.

What I did, what I saw
I leave to you because I have to.

Call me Viv, call me Vivian.
Call me anything.

AFTERWARD

What I Know About Vivian

Few artists have been subject to as many romanticized narratives as Vivian Maier. I have to acknowledge the implied intimacy when I use her first name. I do feel obliged, however, to comment on some aspects of Vivian's life and practice that took shape in the writing of these poems. The story of Vivian Maier's 140,000 plus negatives and prints, Super 8 films and audio tapes discovered in a Chicago storage locker auction has been told many times. Maier died in poverty in 2009; her prints were being sold for upwards of $5000 USD less than a decade later. When the story first broke, the media billed her as the mysterious, self-taught nanny-photographer, a savant who seemingly came from nowhere. The story is no longer that simple thanks to research that has come out since, but there are still "wince-worthy" lapses as Andrea Scott noted recently in *The New Yorker.*

Even the parts of Maier's story that are true are suspect—not the facts themselves, but the context and the impulse to create a mythology from the traces she left behind. Vivian Maier was born in New York in 1926. Her parents, Charles and Marie, were both immigrants from France. They married in 1919 but split up before the 1930 Census. Vivian lived with her mother while her brother, Karl, went with their father. Karl led a difficult life and eventually was admitted to a psychiatric hospital, followed by his death as a patient in a rest home in 1977.

Accounts of Maier's story give little space to issues of class. Vivian's early life was full of what today would be called intersectionalities: being female, poor, and a child of immigrants in a lone-parent family. This kind of language is politely sociological. It barely reflects the actual lives of individuals, the impact of the Depression that hit three years after Vivian was born, the great internal diaspora captured in the photographs of Dorothea Lange and others, and the destitution in large cities.

Vivian and her mother escaped the worst of those years when they returned to her mother's home village in the Champsaur Valley in France in 1932. There she was remembered as "a pretty, blue-eyed, blond six-year-old who at first spoke no French and clung to her mother's side" and "the girl with a bike and a camera" (see Notes). Vivian and her mother returned to New York in 1938, narrowly missing the war in Europe. These life-defining realities go deeper than the Mary-Poppins-with-an-edge character that Vivian is often portrayed as. Children see and remember. Shifting between countries, languages, families, and communities, much of Vivian's early life was spent in a kind of serial statelessness. Perhaps the independence and force of personality she is famous for comes down to a drive for survival learned at an early age.

When Vivian went back to Champsaur in 1950 to settle a modest inheritance, she was taking pictures with a Brownie box camera. She returned to New York in 1951 and bought her first Rolleiflex with its iconic square format images in 1952. She settled in Chicago in 1956. Maier's story is more than a treasure hunt with dodgy meetings in warehouses and a briefcase packed with negatives flown to Canada (both of which happened). The real quest is the uncovering of the work and its validation. It's a story of the resistance and hope of the artist that resonates in our own undiscovered selves. We know just enough to be able to project ourselves into her landscape. This is more than a conceit. We share what psychologists would call a phenomenological knowledge of Vivian Maier's life. There are things we know about her choices, her gaze, and what attracted her whether it was beautiful or not, because we recognize it in ourselves and because we are human. As a poet, I have to believe that this kind of knowledge is as valid as any other. In much of what has been written about Vivian, there is an implicit hope that art somehow freed her—a drive we see in her because we recognize it in ourselves. Our guesses are as much evidence as there will ever be on the matter but they can't be discounted.

Much is made of how a "mystery nanny" managed to carry on a double life under the noses of her employers. My friend, Shelley Banks, a journalist, photographer and poet, points out that caring for the children of the wealthy has been one of the main means of survival of poor, working class women for centuries, so how could we not see Maier's life as anything but typical of the millions before and after her? And why wouldn't those millions have other abilities and ambitions? Is it really so strange that Vivian's employers, who come across as intelligent and perceptive people, knew so little about her photography? As Banks put it, Anne and Charlotte Brontë worked as governesses—does anyone imagine they discussed their novels with their employers?

An old professor of mine said when you are in a counseling session and the conversation isn't making sense, don't listen to what the people across from you say, listen to the music of the transaction. It's a sample of their lives. One watches the interviews with the families Maier worked for and the regard, and even the tolerance Maier was afforded, are clear. It's evident in John Maloof's documentary, *Finding Vivian Maier,* and elsewhere. There are boundaries of family that cannot be transgressed, however, and these are clear as well. One can never be sure what was left on the editing floor, but the music I hear is that of the relationship between employer and employee. And when Vivian says only half-joking to her employer's family that they should adopt her, she must have been aware that she was an outsider in other people's home and the trajectory she was on. In Robert Frost's poem, "The Death of the Hired Man," the farmer's wife says famously, "Home is the place where, when you need to go there, they have to take you in." Unlike Frost's hired man, Vivian had no such a place.

Vivian was tough because she had to be. Still, there is a tension between objectivity and warmth in her photographs of children. These are character studies in which the identity of the child is respected. One of her most iconic images is a young African American boy wearing Mickey Mouse ears. He looks directly into the camera from the window of what is presumably his father's car. It is a study of the American dream. In those eyes we see the child that is and the question of what lies ahead. The critique is undeniable, but the child behind it is an equal part of the story. The two young twins in Florida in matching dresses and hats seem to be caught in half-pose and the kind of attention twins must be used to. Perhaps they weren't quite ready, but the photograph captures a look of skepticism or maybe the kind of forbearance one isn't used to seeing in a child. There's also that image of that young boy with coke-bottle glasses, with a striped tie and an oversized magazine tucked under his white Sunday shirt. He's dressed the way we imagine his father must dress. Like that image of the boy wearing Mickey Mouse ears, the photo seems to embody the trajectory of a future life.

One of the essential qualities of beauty is its ability to make us pause before it. It arrests our attention. There is beauty in these pictures and often a sense of familiarity and undisguised tenderness. It isn't clear who shot the Super 8 film of Vivian and her Highland Park charges picking strawberries in the grassy ravine they liked to go to. Vivian seems unguarded in one of the few truly intimate images we have of her. When the Gensburg boys grew up, they continued to help Vivian in her later years as her health deteriorated. In a moving gesture and perhaps a sense of filiality toward a difficult life, they scattered Vivian's ashes in the same wooded ravine where they picked the strawberries.

John Berger said that Art and art galleries are the domain of the privileged. Vivian never showed her photographs. In the mid-1950s, when Diane Arbus was taking classes from Lisette Model at The New School in New York, Vivian was already starting to amass her defining body of work. The default explanation for why Maier's work was never exhibited is her quirky, abrasive character combined with the fact that she was very guarded about the work itself. This was surely a factor, but how much does it really explain? Vivian was not naive. She had access to some of the best galleries in the U.S. and even has a photograph of Salvador Dali on the steps of the Museum of Modern Art. She seems to have read voraciously and many have commented on her confidence and fearlessness. Vivian knew what she was doing and what was going on in the Art world and the world at large. Given her background, she would have had almost no chance of going to art school, to find a mentor, or to walk into a gallery with a portfolio. She was one of the first women to do street photography and that, in itself, would be enough to close some doors. This doesn't explain everything, but it's a very formidable wall to get past and one that's particularly daunting for someone who didn't have the life chances of her contemporaries, male or female.

One of the now-adult children in Maloof's documentary says Vivian would have been horrified at the idea of others handling her work. She would have been right to worry. When the linguistics professor in the film calls her French accent "an affectation," he is figuratively and literally denying her voice. There are, in fact, other explanations for the accent, but the whole episode can be read as a metaphor for Vivian's life. Whatever care those who own her work now may take, whatever scholarship offers or even these words, she has had no agency in any of this—not the selection of the images, the dodging, the cropping and framing, the tours, the sales, nor the display of her subjects. She has no voice in her legacy.

I like to remember that given a modest inheritance and a chance, Vivian bought her first professional camera, travelled across the States and Canada, and took an extended trip around the world in 1959 and 1960. She was a feminist and that strangely American pejorative, "a liberal," who sympathized with the civil rights movement and photographed in nearby black communities down the road while the families she worked for were at the beach. Despite her abrupt manner she would comfortably engage with the street people she photographed. The children remember her as being generous with her change and she would tell homeless men where they could find a shelter. There are night photographs, scenes with weather and nature, meditations on light and shadow, and a large, rarely shown subset of images from her travels. It is fair to ask how she managed to accomplish what she did, but the newspaper cut-lines and on-line promos often say more about journalists and copywriters than they do about the person that was. Perhaps the word "mystery" should take a hiatus.

Vivian is called a street photographer. A physical street doesn't have to appear anywhere in such work to earn the name. Nick Turpin, the UK photographer, says street photography is not reportage; it is about issues of life in general. It is about the photographer seeing and reacting. He says, "…they know what it feels like to take a great shot in the same way that the archer knows they have hit the bull's-eye before the arrow has fully left the bow." Think of the number of times Vivian must have known with certainty that she had a good photograph among the thousands of shots she never developed or printed. Maybe she simply took the shot and moved on. Somehow though, she must have felt the weight of all that work waiting to see the light of day.

Turpin speaks of the photographer's empathy and loss of self in the moment. This is a photographer's observation and it tells me something about Vivian that others cannot. While some narrators may be reliable, others clearly are not—especially the adults she worked for. The grown children's recollections seem more reliable and unguarded. Their contradictions—the light, the slightly off, and hints of a troubling dark side—have the ring of truth.

It has been said that Maier was not just photographing the street; she was documenting her own life. Art is the space where the artist can be most fully herself. It doesn't seem like a stretch to think that Vivian saw some of those lives she photographed as close to her own. Diane Arbus said those who live on the margins "wear no mask." Maier's photographs often capture her famous or middle-class subjects in the moment before the mask goes up. But there is no disguise for those homeless and exhausted men sleeping on benches or for the hawkers trying to scrabble together a living at Chicago's Maxwell Street bazaar. Maier validates these lives; they are worthy of art—and not the voyeuristic kind. We shouldn't have any illusions about the fact these subjects understood what was going on. There were other photographers on Maxwell Street, in parks and the streets of New York, and they would have been used to it. Maier's photos are free of judgment. It is not such a leap to imagine that many of her subjects had a sense of who Maier was, a mutual recognition that allowed her into their lives if only briefly.

Vivian Maier worked at her craft. Although she had the printing done commercially later on, there is also a photograph of all her developing chemicals arranged on a crowded picnic table. This is essentially a self-portrait. Pamela Bannos says in *A Photographer's Life and Afterlife* that Maier used many cameras, not just the Rolleiflex she is famous for, and that she cropped her work. Maier also had a passion for movies. When Kodak's Super 8 movie camera came out in 1965 and turned personal filmmaking into a cultural phenomenon, the film labels show she bought one within months of when they became available. The Super 8 was the first amateur movie camera to provide the commercial 24/second frame rate. Maier produced many audiotapes as well. She knew the technology. Like any artist, she used it as soon as she could get it.

I am not the first to say it would be impossible to become an artist of Maier's caliber without a critical "take" on her own work. Much is made of the volume of her collection. This shouldn't be a surprise. The 140,000-plus negatives, prints and the other items are entirely in keeping with what one would expect from a serious photographer. This is what artists do. We keep huge volumes of work in our libraries, computer drives, drawers, studios and sheds. It is the physical affirmation of what we do and a kind of fortification against its disappearance.

Bob Carnie, a gallery owner and master printmaker in Toronto, pointed out how absolutely resourceful Maier must have been to keep her work together through all her moves. One of the pleasures of Maier's work is not just the people portrayed, but also the signature of place. Carnie has printed the work of professional photographers specializing in cityscapes and says that that Maier's urban images compare with the best he has seen. Over coffee in a Chicago restaurant, Ron Slattery, who was the first to buy Vivian's prints, said that she applied techniques she learned photographing mountains in Champsaur to her New York and Chicago skyscapes.

In those in-between moments of human indecision that Vivian captures so well, there is a precise sense of the environment and how people exist in these spaces—a seedy parking lot, the beach at Coney Island, a vacant train station, or a school sports day.

The signs in the background deliberately frame the story and its counterpoint. In other images of gutters and windblown streets, there is a well-developed vocabulary. The glimpse of a headline in a newsbox becomes a critique of the folly that produced it. A scrap of paper discarded among remnants of melting snow on a suburban sidewalk has the effect of a tone poem in which the aloneness of the image-maker is part of the scene. Photographs where Vivian includes her shadow assert her presence and the act of seeing while placing the viewer in the same vicinity. In all those portraits of herself in mirrors and shop windows, Vivian is making a gesture toward herself and us. She plays with duality and seems to be making an open-ended inquiry into her own existence and ours as well.

Maier was a documentarian. Only a few photographs from the dreadful year, 1968, have been published. In the six-month period from March until August, the world witnessed the assassinations of Martin Luther King and Robert Kennedy, and the disastrous Chicago Democratic Convention. It is said to be one of Maier's most prolific years and that her work took a darker turn about that time. The worry and grief and the body language in Vivian's photos of the aftermath of the riots and demonstrations in 1968 are still with us. Leonard Cohen said that if you put song into the air and it is still there twenty years later, it means the song is true. This is a test that Maier's work has passed.

Vivian Maier became a tragic figure in her last years—frail, living in poverty, a victim of falls, and unable to pay the rent on her five storage lockers. I would like to believe that her work consoled her in some way, but that would simply be one more narrative. One can imagine a less noble story, one that acknowledges her exhaustion and that she was fully aware both the mass and the worth of what she had produced and sensed its impending loss. It's a miracle that it was saved at all.

Writers and critics have speculated on her sexuality. The fact is we know almost nothing about this aspect of Vivian's life. Her legacy is not helped by theories in search of information that cannot be had. Sometimes the art has to be enough. Her photos of undressed mannequins and their jumbled torsos and limbs heaped in storefront windows have raised some questions; and yes, mannequins are designed to evoke a certain eroticism and can be read as such. It seems to me, however, that the most obvious reading of this work is a pro femina critique of the social construction of beauty, sexuality of course, consumption, transience, waste, and the illusions we live with. This kind of reading is well within her vision and the human landscapes she portrays. Her mannequin images are clearly playing with surrealism; there is violence in the random, disembodied parts as well. She captures raunchy marquees of adult movie houses. Men look at them furtively and seem put off by the woman taking their picture, which was the kind of shot Vivian liked to get and may have provoked. At other times, the emptiness and human absence in front of these places speaks in its own way. There's an exhaustion of the spirit insinuated in the flat light.

When an artist has something that works—really works—they tend to make more of it. Vivian Maier developed a whole "vocabulary of strokes" with regard to the human body. The poems in this volume include a longer work based solely on her photographs of legs in which the part represents the whole. The most recent book, *The*

Color Work, includes a picture of a woman's legs seen from behind. The frame is confined the space between the hem of her coat and the ground, a red shoe on one foot and a cast on the other (p.65). This is followed by another photograph of the vulnerable, nyloned feet of an exhausted woman lying on a stone bench (p. 67) in a narrative of fatigue and anxiety that isn't easily dismissed. Flipping the pages, one sees how truly expressive the torso, hands, and legs are in Maier's work. They are all that's required to evoke the whole figure. The beauty of it, as "Vivian" says in a poem, is that people don't object when you take pictures of their legs. These are subjects that are open to her. Compare the unconscious gestures of living figures in her black and white work and the colour photos of mannequins and it all seems to be part of a wider frame, a broader approach to the human figure. We have to step back to see it.

As for Vivian herself, it may be that no conclusion is possible. In a documentary of the times, Hilda Gore is standing in front of the Vietnam Memorial Wall holding a photograph of her husband that she is about to place there. Facing the camera she says, "When you see a photograph of a person you can love that person." This simple but moving resolution is what I take from Vivian's work. I have her say it in one of the poems because I believe it to be true. Perhaps it's what Vivian hoped for in all those reflections repeated in windows and mirrors, in her own shadow, or in that other self, captured in one of the Super 8 films: an eye-catching woman in an elegant red coat stands in front of a house smashed by a Crystal Lake tornado. The woman raises her Super 8 as she stretches to see in a window, a spy just like Vivian, so intent on her business she doesn't notice we're here.

Notes

Language—the poems use language and idioms current at the time the photographs were taken, primarily from the 1950s through early 1970s. Maier continued to photograph into the 1990s.

"Human River"—"domestic" is after Rainer Maria Rilke's famous poem, "Der Panther" (The Panther).

"Maxwell Street"—is inspired by various sources; in particular, Ira Berkow's, *Maxwell Street: Survival in a Bazaar* (Doubleday, 1977), including the Rooftop Brown story and Sidney Goldstein's comment. Vivian photographed Arvella Gray, who played his steel guitar and sang blues, stomp, and folk on Maxwell for many years. His only album, *The Singing Drifter,* has been reissued by Conjuroo and can be found on-line at http://www.conjuroo.com/. His photograph is on p. 137 of *Vivian Maier: Out of the Shadows.*

The Chicago Defender—mentioned in "Maxwell Street" and "To the 12,000 Unmarked Graves Under Lincoln Park", was a newspaper founded in 1905 directed to African American readers. It greatly influenced the migrations from the south. In speaking about his book, *The Defender,* Ethan Michaili says that it wasn't so much that conditions in Chicago were better than elsewhere, but the spirit of empowerment and resistance reflected in the paper that inspired and attracted people to the city.

1968—Studs Terkel's prescient quote, which opens this section, is from his radio documentary, *This Train,* recorded on one of two trains travelling from Chicago to the March on Washington, August 27-28, 1963. Terkel's broadcasts are available on-line from the Chicago History Museum's Studs Terkel Radio Archive, http://studsterkel.wfmt.com.

1968—Roger Wilkins' "He was in charge..." quote referring to Mayor Richard J. Daley is from an interview in "Chicago 1968", the PBS *American Experience Series,* in a look back on the disastrous Chicago Democratic Convention.

"Watching Us"—Vivian Maier took young Inger Raymond, who was in her care, to Grant Park where anti-Vietnam war demonstrators were camped out a during the Democratic Convention. The description of the "...eerie radiance at night" in the 2nd stanza is adapted from the Roger Wilkins interview noted above.

The poem "children/she cared for..." is partly found from *Vivian Maier: Out of the Shadows* (Cityfiles Press), text by the editors Richard Cahan and Michael Williams.

"The 12,000 Unmarked Graves in Lincoln Park"—All of Chicago's early residents were buried in a single cemetery with 35,000 graves under what is now Lincoln Park and some of the city's most valuable commercial property. Artist Pamela Bannos attempts to uncover layers of the story in her project, *Hidden Truths: The Chicago City Cemetery & Lincoln Park* (http://hiddentruths.northwestern.edu/home.html). While about two-thirds of the graves were moved as the city grew, Bannos estimates that about 12,000 unmarked graves are still there. There is some poetic license in the poem since most Chicagoans would have only been vaguely aware, if at all, of cemetery's history.

What I Know About Vivian, Maier in arriving in France—the first quote is from Marvin Heiferman's essay "Lost, Then Found: The Life and Photographic Work of Vivian Maier," in *Vivian Maier: A Photographer Found*, p.13. The second quote, "a girl with a bike..", is from *Vivian Maier: Out of the Shadows* by Richard Cahan and Michael Williams, p. 15. Publication details are provided in the bibliography.

"What is Street Photography?"—Nik Turpin's discussion is retrieved from IN-PUBLIC. http://www.in-public.com/information/what_is, published in 2000.

BIBLIOGRAPHY (Selected)

Vivian Maier Photographs

Vivian Maier: Street Photographer. John Maloof, editor. Introduction by Maloof and a foreword by Geoff Dyer. Brooklyn, NY: powerHouse, 2011. ISBN 978-1-57687-577-3.

Vivian Maier: Out of the Shadows. Chicago, IL: CityFiles, 2012. ISBN 978-0978545093. Edited by Richard Cahan and Michael Williams.

Vivian Maier: Self-Portraits. John Maloof, editor. Brooklyn, NY: powerHouse, 2013. ISBN 978-1-57687-662-6.

Eye to Eye: Photographs by Vivian Maier. Chicago, IL: CityFiles, 2014. ISBN 9780991541805. Edited and with text by Richard Cahan and Michael Williams.

Vivian Maier: A Photographer Found. London: Harper Design, 2014. ISBN 9780062305534. Edited by Maloof with text by Marvin Heiferman and Howard Greenberg.

The Color Work. New York City: Harper Design, 2018. ISBN 978-0062795571. With a forward by Joel Meyerowitz and text by Colin Westerbeck.

Biographies, Books About Maier

Vivian Maier: A Photographer's Life and Afterlife. Chicago: University of Chicago, 2017. By Pamela Bannos. ISBN 978-0226470757.

Vivian Maier Developed: The Real Story of the Photographer Nanny. Brooklyn, NY: powerHouse, in press at this writing. By Ann Marks. ISBN 978-1576879030.

Vivian Maier Films

Vivian Maier: Who Took Nanny's Pictures (2013) – directed by Jill Nicholls, produced by the BBC, 2013. (https://www.veoh.com/watch/v70590131KFPFjY7N).

The Vivian Maier Mystery (2013). Re-cut and released in the U.S.

Finding Vivian Maier (2013). Directed by John Maloof and Charlie Siske

The Woman in the Mirror (2017). Directed by Ryan Alexander Huang, biographical short film. May be viewed at IMDb.

Other Sources

The Singing Drifter (Blind Arvella Gray). Available from Conjuroo Records, 2005.

Birkow, Ira. *Maxwell Street: Survival in a Bazaar.* Doubleday, 1977. An extensive look at the cultural crossroads at Maxwell and Halsted Streets that gave birth to this remarkable bazaar and birth place of the Chicago Blues.

Studs Turkel Radio Archive. Over 1200 of Terkel's CFCF radio programs including his documentary on the March on Washington cited in the "1968" poems. The CFCF rebroadcast may be found at: https://www.wbez.org/shows/wbez-news/studs-terkels-1963-train-ride-to-washington/a2dc75ea-2529-40f2-b801-46ac4d04e1d4.

Halsted Street USA (1995). This David Simpson film narrated by Studs Terkel retraces the route taken for almost 400 miles by Conrad Friberg's 1934 film, *Halsted Street,* which documents the communities of the Americam melting pot during the heart of the Depression, and travels through scenes Vivian Maier would have known. From Panacea Pictures, on-line at http://www.folkstreams.net/film-detail.php?id=237.

Acknowledgements

I wish to acknowledge the generosity and conversations with those who provided insight into the life and work of Vivian Maier, and whose advice has been an important part of this manuscript. This is includes conversations with Ron Slattery, the first to post Maier's photos on-line; Pamela Bannos, whose in-depth study of Maier's life and work helped to ground the character that appears in these pages; and Bob Carnie, a Toronto master photographic printmaker who shared his insights on Maier's work. I also wish to thank writers Barbara Klar and Shelley Banks for their comments and conversations during the writing process, and Brenda Schmidt, who edited the final manuscript.

The Saskatchewan Arts Board supported the travel and research in Chicago that has been so essential to the writing. Thanks as well to Dean Bauche for his original cover art. As always, I owe a lot to my fellow members of The Poets Combine for the keen eyes they brought to many of these poems.

Bruce Rice Bio

Bruce Rice is the Saskatchewan Poet Laureate, an essayist and editor. He has received the Canadian Authors Association Award for Poetry and two Saskatchewan Book Awards including the Poetry Award for *The Trouble With Beauty* (Coteau) and a Book of the Year nomination for *Life in the Canopy* (Radiant Press). *The Vivian Poems* is his sixth book of poems for adults. He has also published a children's book. The CAA judges said that he "portrays life's hardships with an elegance and simplicity of language which is stunning." Often inspired by art, Bruce writes about individual lives, community and how we are transformed by landscape even as we leave our footprints on it. Bruce lives in Regina, Saskatchewan on Treaty 4 Territory and the homeland of the Métis.